Carys Hannah (formerly known as Carys 'Matic' Jones) is a Birmingham-based poet, musician, and educator. She has headlined numerous spoken word events and performed at several festivals in the UK and South Korea, including Evidently, Wordsmiths, Mouths Wide Shut, Howl, Shambala, Boomtown, and the Gwangju World Music Festival, and has written for the publications Blues and Soul Magazine, Culture M, Eloquence, and Groove Korea. Her work has been showcased on BBC Introducing, OHTV, and The Word is Bond. In 2015, Carys took her autobiographical one-woman show Professional Nomad to the Edinburgh Fringe festival where she won the Hammer and Tongue slam and progressed to the national finals at the Royal Albert Hall. Carys is the founder and former host of Lyrically Minded, an open mic based in Seoul. She has also released an experimental hip hop album, and plans to record more music in the future. Her poetry has been described as 'rhythmic', 'magnetic', and 'courageous'.

HOME

I once found refuge in the arms
of a person who told me that my body felt like home.
I nested in the house of lies they'd built for us
until it was bulldozed to the ground
with me trapped inside
and still I tried
to rest my head on the rubble.
It took some time for me to admit to myself
that rocks aren't pillows.
And so began my self-evacuation,
my quest for emancipation.
I returned to my motherland with some expectation
that I could replant myself in my home soil
but the ground had become too alkaline
and no longer nourished my roots.
Every concept of 'home' I previously knew
had been felled or demolished.
Nowhere felt safe anymore.
Nowhere felt cosy.
Now I'm living out of a backpack,
carrying the weight of the world on my shoulders,
gradually offloading my baggage.
I am of no fixed abode,
drifting across borders and time zones,
and for once
I am settled.
I am home.

Broken Compass

Carys Hannah

Burning Eye

BurningEyeBooks
Never Knowingly
Mainstream

Copyright © 2018 Carys Hannah

The author asserts the moral right under the Copyright, Designs and Patents Act 1988 to be identified as the author of this work.

All rights reserved. No part of this publication may be reproduced, stored in a retrieval system, or transmitted, in any form or by any means without the prior written consent of the author, nor be otherwise circulated in any form of binding or cover other than that in which it is published and without a similar condition being imposed on the subsequent purchaser.

This edition published by Burning Eye Books 2018

www.burningeye.co.uk

@burningeyebooks

Burning Eye Books
15 West Hill, Portishead, BS20 6LG

ISBN 978-1-911570- 34-9

Broken Compass

CONTENTS

Home	9
Dragons	10
The Woman in Koh Lanta	12
Sisyphus	13
(Un)Medicated	14
My Music	16
Sheets	18
Four-Page Spread	19
Con-Mari	20
Clichés	21
Embers	24
Puzzle Box	25
(Porno)Graphic Artist	28
Deep Cuts	30
Trump Card	32
Something	33
Kyphosis	34
If This, Then That	35
Deluded Minds	36
Power-Chord Couple	38
Reclaim the Walls, Part I	39
Reclaim the Walls, Part II	40
The Last Time I Saw You	41
Art Therapy	42

In My Night Stand Drawer	43
Dental Problems	44
A Run-In with the Koh Tao Traffic Police	45
Choking on My Gestures	46
Focus on the Moon	47
Superhero	49
Complex Character	51
Sometimes	54
Acknowledgements	55

DRAGONS

He believes in dragons.
They're currently his favourite animal.
Last month it was tigers.
Three days ago, I marked his science test paper.
Question five: *Name four living things.*
His answers:
1. Dog
2. Cat
3. Tree
4. Dragon

I hastily scrawled *dragons aren't real*
in the margin
whilst awarding him full points
on a technicality.

The red ink stained my palms like blood
the moment my pen hit the paper.
I had become Lady Macbeth
and all the perfumes of Arabia
could not sweeten my little hand.
I'm employed to facilitate the broadening of young minds.
How dare I tell this eight-year-old boy
that dragons don't exist?

Now we're in the classroom.
I hand back every test paper apart from his
and tell him I want to see him after class.
His nostrils begin to flare
and I know that if I gave him back his paper now
he'd screw it up into a ball
and use it as kindling to further fuel his fire.

After convincing him that he's not in trouble
(and bribing him with stickers)
I finally get him to agree to stay behind at the end of the lesson

but he still insists on lining up with the other kids
before pulling up a chair next to my desk.

I get out his science test paper.
I refer to question five,
complete with my scribbled-out annotation.
I point out the glaring error.
'I'm sorry,' I say.
'I made a mistake.
We all make mistakes sometimes, even teachers.'
'That's OK, miss. I think you're a good teacher,' he says.
'Thanks,' I say.

'Hey, miss?
Didn't you say your dad comes from Wales?'
'Yes, that's right.'
'Oh, I love Wales. I've never been there
but I've heard it's beautiful.
There are mountains and valleys
and lots and lots of dragons!
Hey, miss?
Have you ever seen a dragon?'

I see the longing for magic in his eyes.
I take a deep breath.
'Yes,' I say.
'I've seen a dragon
and it was magnificent.
But do you know what?
Not everyone can see them.
I guess I must be really special, like you.'
He smiles, contented with my answer.
I'm teaching him maths, English, and science.
He's teaching me to believe in dragons again.

THE WOMAN IN KOH LANTA

We met five days after Christmas.
You offered me half a joint
and a banana pancake.
We talked about Monsanto
and Neil deGrasse Tyson.
I liked you instantly.

On New Year's Eve
we wrote each other
love notes in the sand
as we watched the paper lanterns
ascend into the night.
Each one a piercing reminder
of the last twelve months
released and burning in effigy.

SISYPHUS

I rise
blurry-eyed,
woken by the sunbeams
that pierce through the sky.
Another day back on the grind,
repeating the cycle,
bored out of my mind.

Trapped in limbo
between chaos and monotony
drilling in my skull
like a frontal lobotomy
but if I surrender to this internal dichotomy
the weight of all I carry
could come crashing down on top of me.

Pushing and toiling
and sweating and striving.
Still holding on
and yet barely surviving.
My hindsight is stronger than my intuition.
Will the seeds that I sow ever come into fruition?

We live in a world of absurdity.
The only thing I'm certain about
is uncertainty
but in every trial
there's a lesson I can take from it
and my reward
is whatever I choose to make of it.

(UN)MEDICATED

Circadian disruption,
discombobulated mental function,
frontal lobe malfunction
not aided by the consumption
of antidepressants.
Personality suppressants.
It's hard to put the past behind you
when it bleeds into the present.
I dug my nails into my skin
to test if I still had feelings
Now every word Trent Reznor wrote
has more significant meaning.
Now I'm peeling back the bandages, revealing
hidden wounds that are still healing.

Some days I just want to feel human.
It's like I'm living a fabricated existence like Truman,
then reality comes crashing down with a thud.
I bit my tongue for so long
all I can taste is my blood,
and they try to fob me off
with therapy and drugs,
but there's no quick-fix solution.
Some days I just need a hug.
Not fluoxetine
or sertraline
or any kind of amphetamine.
I'm tired of living a scripted life
projected onto a movie screen.
But now I'm coming clean
and severing the stage curtain cord,
because people like us
aren't always found on a psychiatric ward.

Backed into a corner
by a plethora
of mental disorders.

A vicious trifecta,
a sinister three-way.
I haven't changed out of my PJs
in three days.
Huddled under sweat-soaked sheets,
earbuds plugged in to binaural beats,
can't face stepping out of the front door,
let alone onto the streets,
wandering and roaming.
Can't fake it or phone in
when my brain's been completely
depleted of serotonin.

An ouroboros pattern,
too deflated to flatten
the face of the bloke who says,
'Cheer up, love! It might never happen!'
and you know he wouldn't say that
to someone of his own gender
and I'm not being overly sensitive or too tender
but I switched my agenda.
Made an appointment to see my GP
back in November,
and through all of the setbacks
and the pitfalls
and the down days
and the duvet days
I have to remember
the meds aren't a sign of defeat or surrender.

MY MUSIC

He's the metronome
that sets the pace
for my heart to beat to.

He breathes life into my ligaments
and every single filament
of my body
starts to glow
and overflow
with energy.
He radiates from me.

He's the kick-drum to my snare.
The bass to my lead,
though the word 'lead'
is mislead-ing
because
I'm driven
by his rhythm.
Like a prism
I reflect the light he's given
to me.

He fills the spaces in the silence,
whispering into my eardrums,
lifting me out of the doldrums.
He is my therapy.
He hums a melody
and I add the harmony
and together we create a symphony.
Our two voices working together
in perfect synergy,
the sum of our components
is far greater than anything
we could produce individually
and it doesn't matter if he's out of key
because to me

he will always be
pitch-perfect.

I tried to study his manuscript
but his score is so magnificently complex
I could never fully get my head around it.
Besides, I've always been better at improvised jazz
than meticulously rehearsed arias anyway.

So I embrace the fact
that there will always be
a degree
of mystery
between him and me
because
every day he surprises me,
he entices me repeatedly.
Drumming syncopated rhythms on my back,
he provides the soundtrack
to my days
with the ways
he alternates between time signatures,
shifting his dynamics,
and he doesn't break boundaries
because as far as we're concerned
no boundaries exist.

He can be
traditional or avant-garde,
classical or contemporary,
underground or mainstream,
major label or indie,
amplified or acoustic.
He is my music.

SHEETS

If these sheets could talk
they would warn me
not to let you under them.

FOUR-PAGE SPREAD

I was in a magazine.
It wasn't enough.
He wanted the cover girl.

CON-MARI

I've spent an entire morning
binge-watching videos
and reading articles
about how folding my bras
can bring me joy.
If only I had known
the key to happiness
was hiding in my underwear drawer
all along,
I could have saved a fortune on therapy.

CLICHÉS

The mutual attraction was there from the get-go,
but you'd been embroiled in a toxic union
and only just let go.
Now, clichés are clichés for a reason,
which is a cliché in itself,
but it has to be said,
I needed to be cautious
for my own emotional and spiritual health.
Possibly more so than yours,
because in your state of fragility
you risked temporarily losing the ability
to view things logically
and I knew it was a bad idea
to get too close to you during this period of vulnerability,
but it turned out I was the naive one,
trying to convince myself
we could continue the relationship platonically.

Still, I tried not to overanalyse or be too pedantic
when the friendship took on a whole new dynamic.
Now I'd been caught by the wave, and I could drown or keep riding it,
but we had too much chemistry, there was no point in fighting it.
And despite my insistence that breathing space was imperative
for us to succeed, you tried to convince me that timing was relative
and we should live for the moment.
Seize the day.
Carpe diem.
I look down at my pen,
and find it's writing clichés all over again.

So then we were walking along blurred lines and it was all ambiguous,
said we weren't doing titles but it felt ridiculous
that society forced us into boxes, so when pressed to label it
I used another cliché, said we were 'friends… with benefits'.

But really, there was more to it.
The intimacy was just one of many facets.

We lived hard.
We laughed hard.
We played hard.
But fuck skeletons in your closet;
you had a whole graveyard.
Opened the door to me slightly,
but I didn't force it.
I knew in due time
I'd discover all of your rotten corpses,
and now my vision of you has become
somewhat distorted and contorted.

The cynic in me never expected it to last.
Said you were trying to move forward
with one foot stuck in the past,
which inevitably caused you to stumble and trip
and fall face-first into your previous relationship.
And whilst she had you by the ankle, you could barely remain standing;
her bed was your crash mat, it provided a soft landing.
You may have history,
but she cannot be your legacy.
You find comfort in the familiarity of her body
when you previously sought refuge in mine.

You found yourself conflicted,
said my kisses were addictive,
but you didn't want to be restricted
and claimed you couldn't make up your mind.
So I made the decision easier for you by removing
one factor from the equation.
In spite of my hesitation, put an end to our liaison.
Overwhelmed by human desire,
this was our baptism of fire,
but it transpired that you required
more than one woman could give you.

Went back to her, but still wanted us to continue.
Unleashed the snake within you.

You thought you were my forbidden fruit?
Nah, you were the serpent in my Eden.
The signs were there all along, but I refused to read them.
Ignored my highway code
and continued driving blindly along this open road,
but I'm getting off at the next exit
and leaving you to decay in your cesspit.

EMBERS

I slept in your T-shirt last night.
I convinced myself it smelled like you,
but in this cynical, sober light
I know it must have been psychosomatic
as I'd put it through the spin cycle
three, six, nine, twelve times,
determined to rinse any trace of you from its fibres.
I found a shoebox full of cards and letters from you
whilst helping my parents move house.
Mum asked me why I hadn't burned them.
I told her it was out of fear
that the embers wouldn't die,
that they would escalate into a towering inferno
and destroy everything I possess
once again.

PUZZLE BOX

He craved love,
yet it terrified him.

Something deep within his core
shut off the moment he returned from war
and was transported back to a world
in which he no longer fit.
Reality became an alien concept to him.

He said he was floating.
Told her that when he met her,
she became his gravity.
She was also floating.
Grabbed his hand for anchorage and stability
and they pulled each other back to Earth
and continued the journey together,
unsure of their destination,
and that was OK.
They could have explored
unknown galaxies together,
rerooted and spawned a new civilisation.

But he'd been pulled apart.
Disassembled.
Dissected into fragments
like a puzzle box,
trying desperately to figure out which pieces fit.
She gave him what he'd been craving.
She loved him with her entire being
in the hope that her love contained the code
to crack the conundrum,
to piece back together this broken puzzle box
of a man.

She was also broken.
Yet she crawled on her hands and knees
picking up the shards of the man she loved,

cutting her fingers to bloody shreds in the process.
In return, he offered her a solid foundation
and gradually helped her to rebuild herself.
Told her he'd be her refuge.
Her hideaway.
Her protection from the world
that had been so unkind to her.
She believed him.

His sleight of hand was so subtle
that she initially didn't notice
when he began to slowly dismantle her,
removing one brick at a time
and carefully stacking them on top
of her increasingly fragile framework
like a giant game of Jenga,
until she could no longer bear the weight
and came tumbling down.
He wanted to break her.
He succeeded.
But he wasn't finished with her yet.

He began to manipulate her,
strategically reassembling her blocks
to form a staircase.
Walking all over her and proceeding to climb
until he'd reached the summit.
He'd reduced her to nothing more than
a series of stepping stones in his eyes,
a means of getting to where he thought
he wanted to be.

But now that he's at the top,
his head's in the clouds
and he's finding himself once again
floating through the atmosphere

with no direction,
lamenting the loss of the woman who once
kept him grounded.
Looking for another damaged structure
to rebuild and destroy.

As for her?
She craves love,
yet it terrifies her.

(PORNO)GRAPHIC ARTIST

She straddles the fine line
between art and pornography
as she straddles the man
who used to straddle me.

Does an intimate act
remain an act of intimacy
if it's captured digitally,
reproduced and rescaled to billboard size,
then hung in a gallery
for the general public to see?

Painted in graphic detail.
Nothing open to interpretation
or left to the imagination.
Brush strokes outline the intricate contours
of their intertwined anatomies.
Her head tilted back in a display of ecstasy.
His face the textbook snapshot of the moment of climax
like an athlete bursting through the red tape
at the finishing line.

It seems that Narcissus has finally found someone
he loves almost as much as his reflection.
How long before I see a projection
of his erection
magnified ten thousand times
and beamed onto the side of a large…
um…
erection?

I swear the Sandman must have tattooed
a replica of the image on the inside of my eyelids
as it's all I can see
when I try to sleep at night.
Their bodies forever burned into my retinas.
The stench of scorching flesh,
the searing pain of the branding iron

will never vacate my memory
and I would willingly pluck my eyeballs
out of their sockets
to stop his semen from dripping
like Chinese water torture.

But once an obscene scene
has been seen
it can never be unseen.

DEEP CUTS

The majority
will eventually
be amongst the marginalised
if our schools,
hospitals
and libraries
are privatised
and the government
keep spitting lies
we criticise
because we're not
playing the victim
but we're still being victimised.

As the seas
of austerity
grow rougher
it's those on the bottom deck
who suffer
as a result of cutbacks
that serve to further
feed the fat cats.
We need to backtrack
and get the banks
to pay some cash back.

Instead we suffocate the masses.
Cut off their air supply.
Deprive them of
essential tools
they need to just get by
as the bourgeoisie
suck out our souls
until the source runs dry.
Binging on
the sustenance,
ignoring hungry cries.

Give us access
to the human right
of knowledge.
Keep our libraries open.
Cut tuition fees for college.
We want what we're entitled to,
not the leftover spillage.
Make education
accessible to all,
not just for the privileged.

TRUMP CARD

This was a freestyle exercise. I was given the words 'accountable', 'pipe' and 'circle'. I improvised this piece and transcribed it without editing.

He says he'll build a wall on Mexico's dime,
he's given the go-ahead for the Dakota pipeline,
he's filled his pockets through corporate crime.
Now he's at an age most would say is past his prime
but he's 'leader of the free world',
which is oxymoronic.
This iconic business tycoon suffers from
a chronic case of bigotry,
he's dragging us down the slippery
slope of no hope,
he's a racist, sexist, homophobic dope
who loves to gloat,
he thinks he's invincible and insurmountable
but we need to unite and hold him accountable.
We want truth, not alternative facts,
and we won't relax
until he shows his tax
returns, but he'll never learn
because he's too narcissistic,
he goes ballistic
at the tiniest bit of criticism,
so we attack him with our witticism
and hit him in the ego
as his cronies circle-jerk around him
and hail him as a hero
but we won't be silenced,
we'll continue to shout
now we're living in the dystopian nightmare
the sci-fi novelists warned us about.

SOMETHING

There's something in the atmosphere.
It's thick like treacle.
It gets under your fingernails
and sticks to your teeth.
It cakes on your skin
like bad foundation.
No one can quite explain exactly what it is
but we all agree
there's something in the atmosphere.

KYPHOSIS

My spine is a fragile support system.
Each vertebra a rung
on a wonky rope ladder
lined by a network of knots.
Muscles contract like balled fists.
Joints click like fingers
at a coffee shop poetry slam.
'Stand up straight,' they say.
I wish I could.

IF THIS, THEN THAT

If bananas, then nuts.
If peppers, then spray.
If raspberries, then gooseberries.
If pomegranates, then dirt.
If apples, then apples.
If artichokes, then resuscitate him.

DELUDED MINDS

How can you see the world
with your eyes half-shut?
Claiming you're open-minded
when you're anything but.
Held back by your prejudice,
you're caught in a rut.
Old habits die hard
but you need to come unstuck
because ignorance breeds ignorance
and hatred breeds hatred,
it transcends generations;
that's what makes me frustrated.
Killing innocence
by planting seeds of evil
corrupted by deluded minds
who say we're made unequal.
Things may have changed since MLK
but people still hate people.
It's like we're trapped in the first volume
and not moved on to the sequel.

Twisted preachers and teachers
and motivational speakers,
sociopaths and leeches
spitting venomous speeches.
We don't need them to reach us
when it's hatred they teach us.
It's essential that we trust
those who seek to enrich us.

Why can't you look at the whole picture?
Just seeing what you want to see
and misquoting scriptures.
Taking them out of context
and creating your own rules,
but if Jesus suddenly returned
do you think he'd be proud of you?

Neo-Nazis masquerading as politicians
say our culture's been polluted,
we're losing sight of our tradition.
Trying to fulfil Enoch Powell's mission,
feeding on the vulnerable,
spreading paranoia and superstition.

We need to look at life
from various perspectives.
Love, compassion, and progression
should be our universal objectives
so we can create a space where every faith,
custom and value is respected
and ultimately no one is marginalised or neglected.
That's all well said and done,
but what's the solution?
Can I leave this open-ended with no conclusion?

POWER-CHORD COUPLE

I kept the rhythm,
you drove the melody.
Strings and keys,
horns and drums,
we co-wrote each other.

We hit a bum note.
I mistook our discord for dissonance.
You no longer played to my beat,
and I was content for you to follow
your inner metronome
as I ad-libbed,
but you had reached your
Herbie Hancock avant-garde phase
and sought out a new Watermelon Woman.

RECLAIM THE WALLS, PART I

It's two o'clock on a Sunday afternoon.
I've barely left my bed when my phone goes off.
I stagger to the other room
where I left it.
It's a girl I know.
More of an acquaintance than a friend.
I think she's pretty cool, though.
She says, 'I don't know if you're busy
and I know we've never really hung out,
but I would appreciate your company
if you happen to be about.
Everything is shit right now
and instead of moping indoors
I wondered if you fancied
helping me to tag some walls?
Wear dark clothes.
I'll lend you a hoodie and some gloves,
oh, and make sure you wear trainers
in case we have to run off.'
I meet her in the underpass
where the council blasted off her last display
(and the two before that).
We face the wall, spray cans in hand,
ready for combat.
She tapes her stencil to the surface,
steps back and prepares for attack,
swoops and takes down one brick at a time,
peels back the acetate to reveal clean lines
imitating those scrawled by a naughty school kid
in dry-wipe pen:
I will not spray paint on this wall again.
I will not spray paint on this wall again.
I will not spray paint on this wall again.

RECLAIM THE WALLS, PART II

I'm a big ball of adrenaline
swooning over my new heroine,
witnessing her redefine
the concept of all that's feminine.

THE LAST TIME I SAW YOU

We went out for Indian food.
You made a point of repeating that you'd prefer Chinese,
but this was my night.

I chose the restaurant around the corner.
You insisted on driving,
even though it was a two-minute walk from my flat.
The tinted windows of your BMW concealed our faces,
whilst the street lamps would have illuminated them.

My previous boyfriend was a mimosa and blueberry pancake
    man.
Brunch was our weekend ritual.
I never knew what you liked for breakfast,
as you were always gone before morning.

ART THERAPY

I fooled myself into believing
that I'd written you out of my system.
That every drop of ink contained your stem cells.
That you no longer resided in my bones.

Three nights ago
you scrawled your name across my ribcage
like a street artist occupying the space they once tagged
and I was reminded that
indelible marker never really washes away.

IN MY NIGHT STAND DRAWER

I have a drawer full of out-of-date condoms,
crumpled receipts,
and unfinished poems about you.
I guess this one will join them
as I have no idea how to end it.

DENTAL PROBLEMS

My tongue is sore
from habitually exploring
the serrated edge of my cavity-riddled molar.
I know I should get it seen to
but I probably won't.
It's not that I'm scared of dentists.
I'm just not good at making appointments.
Or sending invoices.
Or anything that involves filing paperwork.
Or picking up a phone.
I fluctuate between anxiety and apathy,
putting things off by forgetting they exist,
then having a panic attack when I remember they do.
I really should get my teeth checked out.

A RUN-IN WITH THE KOH TAO TRAFFIC POLICE

On the island of turtles
I narrowly avoided
being strip-searched
at the side of the road,
no thanks to my companion
who had forgotten
to throw away his roach.
(I wasn't smoking.)

CHOKING ON MY GESTURES

When good intentions boomerang
and grip me by the windpipe
I retreat until I get my breath back.
I've been hibernating for a while.

FOCUS ON THE MOON

I clutch my bag of groceries like a weapon,
wrap the handles around my fingers like a knuckle duster.
Clenched fists have become my natural stance for every solo
    moonlit walk.
I'm prepared when he enters my peripheral radar.
My neck remains rigid,
fingertips echo pale joints.
He's shadowing my every step from across the street.
'Hey! Hey, sexy!'

Focus on the moon.
Tune in to the sound of evening traffic.
'Hey! I'm talking to you! Do you want to go for a drink with me?'
'No!'

Keep focusing on the moon.
Notice how it's not quite a waxing crescent.
Resist the temptation to stare at your feet.
Fight the desire to scream in his face.
'You don't want to go for a drink with me?'

Keep focusing on the moon.
Notice how the clouds frame it like a halo.
'What's your name?'
'Leave me alone.'
'Fuck off.'

Keep focusing on the moon.
'Hey, where do you live?'
'Stop following me. Stop talking to me. I am not interested.'
'Fuck you, bitch.'

Keep focusing on the moon.
Let it become your compass.
The bigger it glows, the closer you are to home.
'Hey, bitch. Are you crazy?'

Keep focusing on the moon.
Battle the urge to yell, 'Yes, I am fucking crazy, so stop it before I
 slice you open from your belly button to your left nostril.'
Instead, yell, 'Are you?
What makes you think it's acceptable to harass women on their
 way home from the supermarket?
Stop it before I call the cops.'

Keep focusing on the moon.
Try not to allow relief to fool you
as you sense him disappear from your peripheral radar
with one last mating call of 'fuck you!'
There could be another around the corner.
You have encountered many like him before.
They are the reason clenched fists have become your natural
 stance
for every solo moonlit walk.

SUPERHERO

This is a passive-aggressive poem of sorts.
Minus the aggressive part.
We both know why I can't relay my thoughts
directly to you at this point in time.
So I'll communicate in the most comfortable way I know how:
from my brain
to my hand
to the pen
to the pad
to my tongue
to the mic
to the airwaves.
Potentially reaching hundreds
with the intention of getting a message to just one.

You know I don't wear my heart on my sleeve.
I wear it emblazoned on my chest
like Superman's 'S'
so the world can see.
And some view it as a mark of vulnerability
making me susceptible to attack
by emotional kryptonite.
But you told me
that it's not a sign of weakness
but a symbol of strength and bravery.
An emblem I should display proudly.

You showed me
I can catch smoking bullets with my bare hands.
Save kids from burning buildings.
Circumnavigate the globe in less time than it takes you to
sneeze.
Even wear my underpants over my tights and still look good.
You always had faith that my potential was limitless
even when I didn't believe it myself.
You taught me that the only thing weighing me down
and preventing me from flying

was my own self-doubt.
You reminded me
that just because we grow up,
it doesn't mean that we have to stop believing in superheroes.

I guess what I'm trying to say
in my roundabout, periphrastic way
is thank you
for being a source of super-empowerment.

COMPLEX CHARACTER

When I was twelve years old
my father was called in for a meeting
with the deputy head teacher at my school.
I recall waiting outside
staring at my feet,
clenching my fists,
squeezing my eyes shut.
Wishing I could be anywhere else.

I could hear raised voices
coming from the other side of the door
and I was thinking,
*Dad, please don't embarrass me or yourself
by losing your temper.*
I already received enough abuse at school as it was
and at the time
I thought my dad was against me
like the rest of the world.
When I came home from school
puffy-eyed,
tears staining my cheeks,
he'd come at me with that 'sticks and stones' bullshit
and tell me not to be so sensitive.
But I knew it hurt him too.
He was as bad at concealing his emotions
as I was.

Eventually, the deputy head called me into her office.
I felt so intimidated by the woman.
She was the kind of person who could make you feel
two inches tall
with just a stare.
Like most teachers,
she had her favourites,
and she made it clear
that I wasn't one of them.

Rather than fulfilling her role
of educator,
counsellor,
and mentor,
she patronised and belittled me
even in front of my dad.
The only thing that set her apart
from the rest of the bullies
was a forty-five-year age gap
and a fat salary.
She tried to justify the behaviour of the other kids
and I'll never forget what she said next.

She turned to my dad,
completely ignoring me
as if I wasn't in the room.
And she said,
'Carys is a complex character'.

Now, I'd never heard that expression before
but I gathered from my father's reaction
that this was the teacher's 'polite' way of saying,
'Carys is awkward.'
'Carys is weird.'
'Carys is a freak.'
'Carys gets what she deserves.'
'Do you even blame those other kids?
If I were twelve, I'd want to spit on her,
kick her,
and set her hair on fire too.'

And yet, I liked the way it sounded.
'Complex character'.
The alliteration was so pleasing to my ear.
'Carys the complex character'.

I tried to shake it off

but the phrase continued to echo
over
and over
and over in my head.
Complex character,
complex character,
complex character,
complex character.

So I made the decision
to ameliorate her words
and use them to empower myself.
Why should this be a negative label?
Complexity is an art.
Complexity is beautiful.
And one of the benefits of growing up in the church
and being force-fed a diet of Bible verses
is that I know that in Psalm 139
David wrote,
Thank you for making me so wonderfully complex.
Even at the age of twelve
I possessed enough self-awareness to know
that I would rather be a complex character
than a clone of all the other kids
and conform to the unwritten rule
that in order to survive at school
you have to ostracise anyone
who has the courage to dare to be
their authentic self.

The deputy head teacher
intended to insult me
when she called me a 'complex character'.
But what she'll never know
is that it was in fact
the biggest compliment she could have given me.

SOMETIMES

Connections.
Reflections.
I need protection
from myself
to stop moving in the wrong direction.

I always follow by habit.
Wasting days
with nothing to show of it.
Got a starting point
with nowhere to go from it.
And this is how I write
and this is how I live.
Sometimes I take
and forget to give.
Sometimes I hate
and don't allow myself to forgive.
Sometimes I don't claim
what's rightfully mine.
Sometimes I allow myself
to be pushed to the back of the line.
Sometimes I accept punishment
when I know I've committed no crime.
Sometimes I panic
when everything's fine.

But that's enough about the 'some' times.
Let's talk about the present times.
The only time that I can change
and move on from unpleasant times.
Even if it's only through my thoughts
and through my rhymes.
Whether it's to elevate myself
or to help humankind,
revolution begins with the mind.

ACKNOWLEDGEMENTS

This has been one of the most difficult parts of the book to write as I have so many people to thank, I'm bound to forget some names.

First, I have to thank my family, especially my parents, Maldwyn and Ruth Jones, for your unwavering support. I hope I've done you both proud and that you're not too embarrassed or offended by the rude bits and the sweary bits.

Huge thanks to Clive, Bridget, Harriet, Liv, and the whole Burning Eye family for taking me on board and publishing my first collection. This has been on my bucket list since I first heard of your beautiful little press four years ago.

Thanks to John Berkavitch, Zena Edwards, Soweto Kinch, Spoz, Ursula Rucker, John Hegley, Pete Hogg, Vanessa Kisuule, Jessica Care Moore, Paula Varjack, Jasmine Gardosi, Nafeesa Hamid, Juice Aleem, James Hershberger, Elliott Ashby, Hannah Gordon, Salena Godden, Matt Abbott, Brian Blackburn, Gwen Atkinson, Maddie Godfrey, Jo Bell, Alexis Satariano-McKenzie, Pritrica Webber, Andrew Webber, Dylan Owen, Kathryn Kettle-Williams, Abby Krausse, Brian Homer, Lizzie Turner, Will Turner, Jasmene Smith-Brown, Alex King, Jocelyn, Libby Richardson, Shaun Southway, Shiun Southway, Kaytee DeWolfe, Sean Thompson, Dann Gaymer, John, Gav, and the rest of Seventh Syndicate.

Finally, I would like to thank everyone who has inspired or supported me in any way (and that includes you reading this right now. Yes, you! You are awesome!). I love you all.

www.ingramcontent.com/pod-product-compliance
Lightning Source LLC
Chambersburg PA
CBHW021000090426
42736CB00010B/1399